"I feel I should warn you . . ."

"I feel I should warn you . . ."

HISTORIC PRESERVATION CARTOONS

Edited by Terry B. Morton
With an essay by Draper Hill

NATIONAL TRUST FOR HISTORIC PRESERVATION

THE PRESERVATION PRESS

The Preservation Press
National Trust for Historic Preservation
1785 Massachusetts Avenue, N.W.
Washington, D.C. 20036

Library of Congress Cataloging in Publication Data

"I feel I should warn you . . .": historic preservation cartoons.

Edited by Terry B. Morton; with an essay by Draper Hill.

1. Historic sites—Caricature and cartoons.   2. Wit and humor, Pictorial.   I. Morton, Terry B.

NC1763.H5122   741.5′9   75-12480
ISBN 0-89133-027-5 (paperbound)   MARC
ISBN 0-89133-028-3 (clothbound)

Printed in the United States of America
89 88 87 86 85   8 7 6 5 4

Designed by Gerard A. Valerio
Printed by Reese Press, Baltimore, Md.

Cover drawing by Saxon © 1969 The New Yorker Magazine, Inc.

*Dedicated to the preservationist, often a lonely vigilante
in a seemingly hopeless cause but one so tenacious over the years
that there is now emerging a preservation profession.
Architect, museologist, editor, craftsman, secretary, historian,
administrator, lawyer—by the thousands they are using their
specific training and experience in local, state and national
preservation work to help safeguard America's
cultural heritage.*

Drawing by Paul R. Hoffmaster; Preservation News, December 1967

Contents

Preservation Cartoons Observed   *page ix*
   TERRY B. MORTON

Forward March?   *page xiii*
   DRAPER HILL

I.

"Whatsoever a man soweth, that shall he also reap."   *page 1*

   GENERAL PRESERVATION CARTOONS

II.

"Our preservation of the past is a responsibility to the future."   *page 57*

   PRESERVATION-RELATED CARTOONS

III.

"Progress was OK. It just went on too long."   *page 73*

   CARTOONS ADDRESSING SPECIFIC PRESERVATION ISSUES

Index   *page 86*

"To arms! To arms! The bulldozers are coming!"

Preservation Cartoons Observed

SOME PRESERVATIONISTS' DREAMS ARE SHATTERED BY THE WRECKING BALL AND THE BULLDOZER. OTHER preservationists are more fortunate; their goals are accomplished slowly over the years, or immediately. This is dependent upon many factors, such as the scope of the goal and conditions mediating for or against it.

Only 20 short years were required to produce this collection of historic preservation cartoons! The goal was not a near impossible one, it was just that the idea was kindled when there were only 10 or 12 preservation cartoons in hand. Time had to pass so that cartoons could be created by National Trust commission for use in its newspaper, *Preservation News*, and its magazine, *Historic Preservation*, or could be reprinted following use in other newspapers and magazines. Thus the cartoons were assembled from various sources over these 20 years, including the Trust purchase of some free-lance cartoons. A selection was made recently to form this collection when there were cartoons sufficient in number and content to make a book.

This is a book intended to entertain and educate the activist preservationist, whether committed and working as a professional or a volunteer, and especially the converted and unconverted American who may never be more than a nominal preservationist. The importance of the nominal preservationist cannot be underestimated, for millions are desperately needed to endorse and support preservation causes—being aware and treasuring the past, respecting and using property wisely, lending a voice, signing a petition, casting a vote and contributing the widow's mite.

The cartoon, like folk music, is light and heavy at the same time and provides a way to lighten the preservationists' burden. It is possible immediately to enjoy the art and the humor and then to accept the pain from a deeper message.

As this book will help attest, landmarks are everywhere and relate to all people. They enhance the environment, represent all building and art types, all time periods, all walks of life and all nationalities that have helped make America. Defined as sites, buildings, objects, structures and districts by the National Historic Preservation Act of 1966, historic properties span the years from prehistoric America to today. They are colonial to contemporary in architectural style and from house to factory in building type. They are large and small; urban, suburban and rural; with and without land, or with just a little. They bear traces of the politician and the poet and influences from Swedish to African. They reflect national development from agriculture to commerce and are of local, state and national importance. They should be omnipresent and aren't, and their numbers should grow each day. Landmarks are created as history is made and another set of cultural resources moves up for identification, evaluation, protection, interpretation and use. Most important, although landmarks generally were made by those now dead, landmarks are for the living, through the continued enjoyment of study and use.

This book represents the interest of an early Trust staff, Helen D. Bullock, Terry B. Morton, Tony P. Wrenn and Patricia Williams, members of the Department of Information. The book idea was nurtured through the years by the subsequent Department of Publications, which in January 1975 became the Preservation Press of the National Trust. The first four preservationists were joined in this goal by Diane R. Maddex and Carleton Knight, III, who in their responsibility for *Preservation News* developed a number of cartoons with Draper Hill. Mark Mannes, a publications summer intern during 1973, spent six weeks at the Library of Congress, searching back issues of the *New Yorker*, the *Saturday Review*, *Punch* and the *Saturday Evening Post*. Sharon Timmons was project editor for *"I Feel I Should Warn You . . ."*.

Trust members and friends have been especially helpful over the years, sending appropriate cartoons. What fun to have returned from lunch one day several years ago to find that a member had left a copy of an old cartoon, but one new to the staff, from *Harper's Weekly*, October 28, 1871 (page xii).

One long-range goal is for historic preservation to be intellectually and objectively integrated into America's national priorities, in the mainstream of education and information. Since often there have been few exact, direct aids for preservation, one pleasure has been finding indirect aids where one might least expect it. This includes the concern of an artist, writer or politician who is sensitive to the past and to the value of historic preservation even though the person's lifework is focused elsewhere. Quoting from the writings of a John Steinbeck or publishing the works of an Alan Dunn helps highlight and summarize an idea with authority and respect and also gives a relevance to historic preservation in the changing social and political scene.

Two cartoonists especially stand out for their special interest in preservation issues and their appreciation of architecture—Draper Hill and Alan Dunn. Mr. Hill has been contributing preservation cartoons since 1969, when the first cartoon he drew for the Trust appeared in the June issue of *Preservation News*, "If an old herd of cows could lay out Boston . . ." (page 58). His professionally executed editorial cartoons helped make our little monthly newspaper seem closer to the big league, more like a big-city daily. Three to four days after a telephone conversation with him, a poignant and often humorous rendering of our verbalization was received—he had grasped and sharpened our vague ideas. His cartoons reveal a clarity and boldness of hand and mind and none more so than that high-strutting drummer girl beating out America's frustrations over next year's Bicentennial celebration (page 66).

Mr. Hill is a graduate of Harvard College and studied under a Fulbright Scholarship at the Slade School of Fine Arts in London. He developed an exhibition during this period on the history of caricature for the Arts Council of Great Britain and was the author of two published biographies on James Gillray, 18th-century caricaturist. In 1969 Mr. Hill was editorial cartoonist for the *Wor-*

cester (Mass.) *Telegram*; he is currently editorial cartoonist for *The Commercial Appeal*, Memphis.

In his essay, "Forward March?", Draper Hill, friend and colleague, gives a historical perspective to American cartooning and historic preservation cartoons especially. Also, more of his cartoons were selected for this collection than from any other artist. Runner-up is Alan Dunn, who gave his blessing and approval to reprint his work for the advancement of historic preservation. Some years ago when Mr. Dunn turned down our request to draw cartoons for Trust publications, he replied that his "thinking time" was overcommitted and gave permission to reprint any of his work. "I greatly admired the copies of *Preservation News* you sent me," he wrote, and "I am always eager to get the preservation message across . . . I do wish I could be of more help."

Thus Mr. Dunn's work was searched for appropriate cartoons and his newest ones were eagerly awaited on the pages of the *New Yorker*, for which he worked from 1926 until his death in 1974, and *Architectural Record*, from 1937. His scene was 20th-century New York City; architecture, which was his avocation, found its way into many of his cartoons. His drawings were not just a record and critique of the architectural style changes that were going on around him but also often a sad but witty comment on the need to reevaluate the past in his ever-changing city.

Other well-known cartoonists will also be found in the book—Charles Addams, Robert Day, Henry R. Martin, George Lichty, Stevenson, Jules Feiffer, Herblock and Charles Schulz. Finally in 1972 when Snoopy discovered the need for historic preservation, our day had come. To have arrived on the daily cartoon page, a national common denominator, in this universally accepted strip meant that historic preservation had come of age and our collection could go to press. However, lest anyone think any preservation project is finished, it is not, and the second collection of historic preservation cartoons is already underway!

Together cartoonists and preservationists are proving that looking backward, to early cartoons for meaning just as to cultural resources from another day, is not a nostalgic escape. It is a practical and meaningful way of moving forward. As Santayana once said to a Harvard class, "Since no man can know how long he will live into the future, it behooves every man to live as long as possible into the past."

Cartoons and historic preservation are meaningful amenities in 20th-century America.

TERRY B. MORTON

The March of Modern Improvement

Drawing by C. S. Reinhart; Harper's Weekly, October 28, 1871

Forward March?

Modern progress shows no reverence for the old or the picturesque. It spares neither the work of human hands nor natural scenery. The romantic old city of Nuremberg is torn down to make way for railroad dépôts, modern shops, and palatial hotels. There was at one time talk of leveling the lofty rock on which stands the castle of Edinburgh, and nothing saved it but the outcry of execration which the proposal roused from a few people of taste. . . .The good people of Boston, who first leveled the breastworks of Bunker Hill to obtain a foundation for the Monument, now talk of abolishing the Monument to give place to stores!

THESE SOMBER REFLECTIONS, WITH THEIR DEPRESSINGLY TIMELESS QUALITY, WERE WRITTEN 103 YEARS AGO TO support a composition by Charles Stanley Reinhart that may well be the granddaddy of American cartoons on historic preservation.

Reinhart's bitter allegorical panorama of destruction and indifference, entitled The March of Modern Improvement, appeared in a supplement to *Harper's Weekly* on October 28, 1871, prominently—if absurdly—advertised as "a picturesque sketch from the upper part of New York." The 27-year-old artist could well have been dispatched to the outer suburban reaches of Harlem for the purpose of drafting a simple exercise in nostalgia. If that was the case, the editors got a good deal more from him than they had requested.

The published wood engraving contrasts a crumbling heritage of 1776 with the stodgy, self-preoccupied bustle of 1871, the date prominently inscribed on the front of the sluggish streetcar. Save for the concern of the agitated elderly gentleman in the left foreground, the demolition of this imposing old house might just as well be taking place on another planet. The severed, truncated remnant of a giant tree—frozen in mid-topple like a desperate, protesting human arm—manages to attract the attention of only three or four tiny figures in the middle distance. Beyond the wreckage, a fresh phalanx of row houses will soon be charging up the hill to block the church and rectory from view. At the far right, another wave of the future is represented by a handsome new palace in the latest approved manner (French Second Empire).

Reinhart's warning is powerful, poignant and unmistakable. (Although he later followed gentler paths of illustration and genre painting, at this point he could hardly have failed to feel the influence of Thomas Nast, whose blockbusting crusade against Boss Tweed and the Tammany

Hall ring was then hitting its climax in the same publication.) As any good cartoon must, the design speaks for itself; it reveals the steel of intellect hardened and polished under the fire of emotion. The author of the accompanying explanation might have missed the point of the young artist's "fine sketch." More probably, as is the editor's occasional wont, the caption writer believed that the message needed some fudging.

The site of the picturesque old mansion, with its Revolutionary traditions, is wanted for a modern building, and down it must go; and with it disappears another of the few links that still connect us with the past. But this is one of the inevitable consequences of progress and improvement. Comfort, cleanliness and convenience are of more importance to society than the merely picturesque, and it is only against the needless *destruction of the memorials of the past that a protest should be entertained. (emphasis added—D.H.)*

The writer goes on to lament the loss of John Hancock's house in Boston as "an act of inexcusable vandalism which can never be repaired." This structure, a dominant landmark and major tourist attraction, had been built in 1735 on the highest peak of Beacon Hill. After a half-hearted defense by concerned citizens and officials which commenced in 1859, the property was acquired by developers in 1863 and razed that summer. The *Harper's Weekly* objection eight years later seems to have been based more on historical significance than architectural merit. The notion that a structure could justify its continued existence on purely aesthetic grounds would not achieve any real foothold for another generation or so. One suspects that Reinhart, newly settled in Manhattan after fine arts training in Paris and Munich, had already reached such a conclusion. In any case, his pioneer effort provides us with an instructive glimpse of the eternal struggle between artistic evangelism and editorial balance.

Over the years, even the most liberal cartoonists have tended to regard innovation and change with a reserve and skepticism that gives them a natural sympathy for the goals of the preservation movement. The drawings in this lively collection were conceived out of a broad spectrum of motives and created for a wide variety of delivery systems, ranging from the old single-sheet copperplate engraving to the modern newspaper comic strip. Produced for the most part over the past half-century, they are by turns angry and sad, activist and passive, realistic and metaphorical, hard sell and soft. The gamut of feeling extends from the muted horror of Gluyas Williams' housewrecker in the act of discovering that he has the wrong number (page xv) to the cold fury of Snoopy's immortal response to the rape of the Daisy Hill Puppy Farm (page 64). There is ample room for the wistful defiance of O'Glass's project for a new brownstone (page 30) and the surrealistic pathos of Chon Day's assault on the synthetic wrapping and marketing of the American promise (page 72).

The Housewrecker Discovers He Has the Wrong Number

Drawing by Gluyas Williams; Copr. 1926, 1954 The New Yorker Magazine, Inc.

Over and over again, a human element is superimposed, warmly and sympathetically, on the sterile wasteland of twisted priorities, highrise miscalculations and counterproductive renewals. It is scarcely surprising that themes and analogies do reoccur from time to time and from place to place, yet the variety and vitality are far more remarkable than any of the parallels. Perhaps the only real common denominator lies in the relentless application of humor to mankind's singularly unfunny propensity for lopping off its roots and fouling its nests. As the stakes rise, so does the urgent need for a universality and lightness of touch, for an alarm capable of reaching and moving the widest possible audience of concerned individuals. George Bernard Shaw once remarked of his habitual recourse to Harlequin's cap and bells, "The real jest is that I am in earnest." Similarly, the effect and appeal of a cartoon often depend as much on the successful camouflaging of purpose and commitment as on the concealment of the amount of time and effort that go into the actual execution.

Cartoons (or caricatures, as they were called before the mid-19th century) have been recognized and employed as potent persuaders for more than 200 years. Even earlier there was a certain loose kinship between architecture and pictorial satire. One of the earliest published caricature attacks on a specific person was a 1651 engraving by Michel Dorigny warning against the taste and practices of the celebrated French architect, François Mansart. In their lighter moments, Leonardo and Inigo Jones dabbled, or rather doodled, in the grotesque. G. L. Bernini, architect of the colonnade of St. Peter's (c. 1667), Rome, and George Dance, designer of Newgate Prison (c. 1780), London, were also famous for their portrait caricatures. Some of the most memorable visual commentaries of our own time are the work of Saul Steinberg, who trained and practiced as an architect before shifting his field. Alfred Bendiner of Philadelphia was a master of both disciplines. This bracketing of talents is neither strange nor paradoxical; each depends for success on a highly developed sense of essence and proportion.

William Hogarth, 18th-century moralist, painter and patron saint of cartooning, was also a perceptive student of decorative taste and architectural style. However, if an edifice collapsed in one of his prints, it was apt to do so in aid of a larger symbolic purpose, such as the exposure of the evils of strong drink or governmental folly. The earliest actual "cartoons" of preservation are probably those drawn by James Gillray during the 1790s. They depicted graphically the grim consequences that Londoners might expect to follow an unresisted cross-channel invasion by revolutionary France. These too were basically allegorical: the tricolor lava of Jacobin democracy threatening the English capital, St. James's Palace in flames, the ravaging and sacking of the Houses of Parliament or the desecration of churches. Some 10 years later, Gillray's friend and rival caricaturist, Thomas Rowlandson, collaborated with another artist on 104 elaborate aquatint views for the ambitious three-volume *Microcosm of London*, published by Rudolph Ackermann in 1808-10. This project was designed to celebrate the architectural glories of the metropolis rather than defend them from menace. Rowlandson also did his part to turn the preservationist of his day into a figure of fun. He was largely responsible for the immensely popular character Doctor Syntax, a progenitor of the modern comic-strip hero, who made his debut in Ackermann's *Poetical Maga-*

zine in 1810. Doctor Syntax was a garrulous old clergyman, pedant and connoisseur of the cult of the "picturesque." His exploits were affectionately portrayed by Rowlandson and chronicled in verse by William Combe. Mounted on his cadaverous nag, Grizzle, Syntax wandered the realm in quest of beauty, expounding interminably on felicities of the wild and rustic landscape and on the infinite charm and instructive character of ancient ruins.

Around the moss-clad walls he walk'd
Then through the inner chambers stalk'd;
And thus exclaim'd with look profound,
The echoes giving back the sound.
  "Let me expatiate here awhile:
I think this antiquated pile
Is, doubtless in the Saxon style.
This was a noble, spacious hall,
But why the chapel made so small?
I fear our fathers took more care
Of festive hall than house of prayer."

The advice Syntax gave was frequently sound, as when he counseled against yielding to fads and crazes in remodeling stately homes.

Why from the solid, simple base
Springs not the column's Attic grace?
. . . .
I think that it should be the aim
Of families of ancient name,
Never from fashion to transfer
Their long establish'd character

By the time that the good doctor returned home from a third and final tour in 1821, the tidy, aesthetic arcadia of his 18th-century world was under siege. Syntax, lost in "untroubled" thought, did not realize London was at hand

Till rising 'bove the cloud of smoke
St. Paul's Dome on the prospect broke

The future—industrialized, mechanized and emancipated—was knocking at the door (and polluting the view from the window). Rowlandson and Combe, aged 65 and 80, respectively, yielded comment to a new generation of satirists, who recorded the mixed marvels of wondrous

LONDON going out of Town. ___ or ___

xviii

The March of Bricks & Mortar!

Drawing by George Cruikshank; From *Scraps and Sketches*, November 1, 1829

inventions, belching factory chimneys, steam transportation and urban sprawl with tempered enthusiasm. Eight years later, the specter of the expanding metropolis took on a malevolent quality in London Going Out of Town or The March of Bricks and Mortar. "Designed, etched & Published by George Cruikshank—November 1st, 1829," the print was one of many to ridicule the current slogan March of Mind, or March of Intellect, then in wide use by politicians and other speech-ifiers as a glowing tribute to democratization and rational progress. (The selection of the title The March of Modern Improvement for Reinhart's cartoon in *Harper's Weekly*, 42 years later, could hardly have been pure coincidence.) Cruikshank's "march" shows a fantastic army of builders' implements—hods, shovels, picks, wheelbarrows, trowels, mallets (and a beer stein or two!)—advancing north on the defenseless hills of Hampstead. Haystacks and livestock flee in terror. Under the hail of new brick, one tree shrieks, "I must leave the field!" Another falls, "mortally wounded." Row upon row of jerry-built "New Streets" of houses that crack before they are finished or rented press the grim offensive. By now, the dome of St. Paul's Cathedral is all but obscured by fumes from a forest of smokestacks, brickworks and limekilns.

The coming of railroads would seem to have done much to shift the emphasis from environmental concern to the preservation of historic buildings as such. Even as cities exploded outward, the relentless iron horse was channeling inward, foraging for living space—*Lebensraum*—downtown. From the 1830s on, London was progressively slashed, penetrated and girdled by tracks and trestles. In the summer of 1863, with a massive new railway bridge preparing to chop its way across the prospect from the foot of Ludgate Hill, Sir Christopher Wren's hard-working masterpiece was once again called into service. On August 8, a *Punch* cartoon and caption urged readers to take advantage of the Last Few Days of St. Paul's.

Now then, make haste, make haste. . . .In a very short time this remarkable edifice will become invisible, owing to the great improvements which the march of intellect and the progress of commerce, providentially force on this Great Metropolis. Therefore, be in time before the view is shut out for ever and ever.... The architecture will well repay inspection, the façade, henceforth to be seen no more, is regarded as one of the finest things in the world, and the majestic appearance of the west front defies at once competition and description. There is no charge. . . .Be in time, be in time.

Four months later, on December 19, 1863, a large, front-page cartoon in the *Comic News* took a broader look at the railroad challenge. The New Scheme For Cutting Up London, as envisaged by C. H. Bennett, heaps the monster's platter with a choice stew of identifiable landmarks, in addition to the inevitable St. Paul's. The Tower of London is impaled on his fork; Leicester Square, Cavendish Square and a projected Thames Tunnel await a fate as possible desserts or savories. Bennett's design reacts, among other things, to the completion of the first subway or

THE NEW SCHEME FOR CUTTING UP LONDON.

Drawing by C. H. Bennett; Comic News, December 19, 1863

THE ART OF RESTORING.

The Original Designer (some few hundred years ago) :—"There— that's my idea of the thing—something quite plain and simple." (*He passes away, together with the few hundred years.*)

The Modern Architect :—"Grand ruin, isn't it? Not enough to restore from? Bless you! I've restored a whole cathedral from a chip of pavement."

"There now, that's about the thing the Original Designer evidently intended—something florid and complicated."

"All you have to do, you know, is to get yourself thoroughly imbued with the *spirit* of the Original Designer."

Spirit of the Original Designer, taking a look round :—"Well, what strange things these moderns *do* design, to be sure. Quite original, though!"

Drawing by J. F. Sullivan; Fun magazine, c. 1877

"underground" in the city, a huge "cut-and-cover" trench that stretched its unsightly arc across 3-1/2 miles of central London.

Once professional cartoonists had, at long last, risen to the defense of cities and to the protection of their architectural treasures, it was only a matter of time before some perceptive wag would address himself, as James F. Sullivan did (around 1877), to The Art of Restoring. Sullivan was a marvelously spontaneous, original comic artist, active from about 1873 to 1894, whose early work for *Fun* magazine was collected in 1878 under the title *The British Working Man, by One Who Does Not Believe in Him*. In 1877, under the heading Institutions Peculiarly English, he drew a second tableau of preservation for *Fun* in which the "prettiest corner of Barnes Common" was staked out as a proposed site for a new sewage works. Sullivan's whimsical essay on The Art of Restoring keeps excellent company with the educational futuristic slide presentation by Jules Feiffer on page 56.

This book does not attempt or pretend to be a history of preservation cartoons. Our selection consists for the most part of drawings by contemporary humorists in the United States, addressing situations that are at least as urgent for us as earlier ones were for Cruikshank, Bennett and Reinhart. I have stressed the important early part undertaken by the English school of cartoonists, who both shaped the art and first came to grips with the specific problem. The magazine *Punch* has continued to play an active role in preservation, particularly under the inspiration and after the example of Fougasse (Kenneth Bird 1887-1965), who served as art editor from 1937 to 1949 and as editor from 1949 to 1952. On our side of the Atlantic, the *New Yorker* has shown a corresponding interest in the subject from its inception a half-century ago. (The magazine was just 16 months old when Gluyas Williams's saga of the errant housewrecker appeared). The casual urgency and high-tensile fragility of Alan Dunn's style became as much of a hallmark to the *New Yorker* as the dry wit and calligraphic economy of Fougasse was for *Punch*. The present collection offers some opportunity to contrast the two national strains of pictorial comedy. It has been suggested that the English spirit is as different from the American "as chalk is from cheese." This distinction might fairly be extended to their respective tastes in comic art if we discount the implication that they cannot be equally appetizing.

Although a great deal has been said in praise of the missionary force of cartooning—"one drawing equals a thousand words" and the like—actual effectiveness is extremely difficult to measure. Cartoons certainly have helped to win some major battles, such as the halting of a planned "adjustment" to the West Front of the U. S. Capitol in 1966. However, most victories tend to be modest ones. A generation or so back, Francis Dahl of the *Boston Herald* managed to remove an information booth eyesore from the Boston Common with a memorable series of gentle shoves. After an alert editorial writer caught Memphis, Tenn., in the act of dumping a choice public morsel of riverside park, Cal Alley summoned up an ardent, evocative vision of the mighty Mississippi that rescued the "damsel" and saved the day.

A comprehensive study of the topic would have to deal with political trial balloons and other

Who Can Be Mean Enough To Break It Up?

Drawing by Cal Alley; The Commercial Appeal (Memphis, Tenn.), May 6, 1953 Reproduced courtesy of Paul R. Coppock

hairbrained, lighter-than-air notions that have been fortuitously punctured in mid-launch. It might also note, with gratitude, the contribution of rough vigilante handbills and fugitive direct-mail pieces like the portrait of a rampaging bulldozer that helped mobilize the citizens of Malibu, Calif., to block an onrushing highway in the early 1960s. Progress comes, if at all, as the result of continuing campaigns of small nips and insistent nudges. The many cartoons that are not dedicated to specific causes serve a larger and even more vital purpose of reflecting and influencing the changing climate of public opinion. From a preservationist viewpoint, the most encouraging circumstance documented by this anthology is the evolution of a limited, elitist urban preoccupation into a matter of broad general concern. If the *New Yorker* sounded the original trumpet charge, Snoopy and the Daisy Hill Puppy Farm represent the heavy artillery. But, don't, please don't, let me deter you with all this purposefulness and militarism. Sir Winston Churchill, tactician, honorary American and card-carrying bricklayer, allowed in 1931 that he had always loved cartoons. He recalled for a *Strand* magazine article,

At my private school at Brighton there were three or four volumes of cartoons from Punch *and on Sundays we were allowed to study them. This was a very good way of learning history, or at any rate of learning something.*

. . . Something indeed—about ourselves, our problems and the pleasant magic of laughter.

DRAPER HILL
Editorial cartoonist

"*Well, anyhow, there'd be no harm in giving it a trial.*"

"Whatsoever a man soweth, that shall he also reap."

— GALATIANS 6:7

Drawing by Louis Dunn; From *The Ultimate Highrise,* © 1971 San Francisco Bay Guardian Books

Drawing by Chas. Addams; © 1970 The New Yorker Magazine, Inc.

2

Drawing by Alan Dunn; From *Architecture Observed*, © 1971 Architectural Record Books

Drawing by Bob Schochet; © 1961 Saturday Review, October 30

"They don't build houses like that anymore."

Drawing by Dennis Renault; © 1964 Saturday Evening Post, September 26

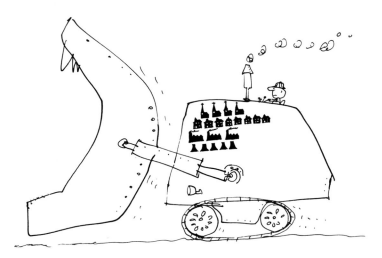

6

"Face it, Charlie. Progress is fifty-per-cent destruction."

"All right, boys, down she comes."

"I'm sure it constitutes no clear and present danger, but it comes off
as one helluva psychological threat."

"The First Hundred Years Are The Hardest, Son!"

Drawing by Draper Hill; Preservation News, August 1968

Drawing by John Ruge; © 1964 Look magazine, August 11

"You're going to love it. It has a charming atmosphere and the food is divine—if it hasn't been torn down."

Drawing by Alan Dunn; © 1966 Architectural Record, March

EEK & MEEK

"I was hoping we could get away from urban renewal problems on this trip."

Drawing by David C. Gerard; © 1970 Parade magazine, July 19

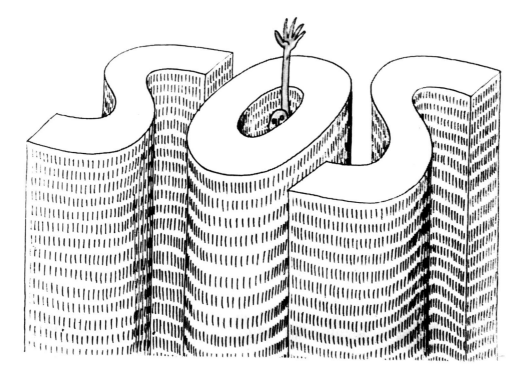

16

"And now I guess this meeting of the Save Our National Landmarks Committee stands adjourned."

ONE IF BY LAND
TWO IF BY SEA
THREE IF BY AIR...

"We Must Become A Nation of Volunteers Again."

Drawing by Draper Hill; Preservation News, April 1970

"For heaven's sake, Martha, admit you're licked!"

Drawing by Jeff Keate; © 1968 National Observer, July 19

"Don't Forget the Tail, Mr. President!"

Drawing by Draper Hill; Preservation News, February 1970

"We should be able to preserve our resources. As they grow less there are more of us to preserve them."

Drawing by F. H. Brummer; Preservation News, December 1970

"The city has the utmost respect for its historical shrines . . .
The whole demolition will be carried out by fully trained craftsmen!"

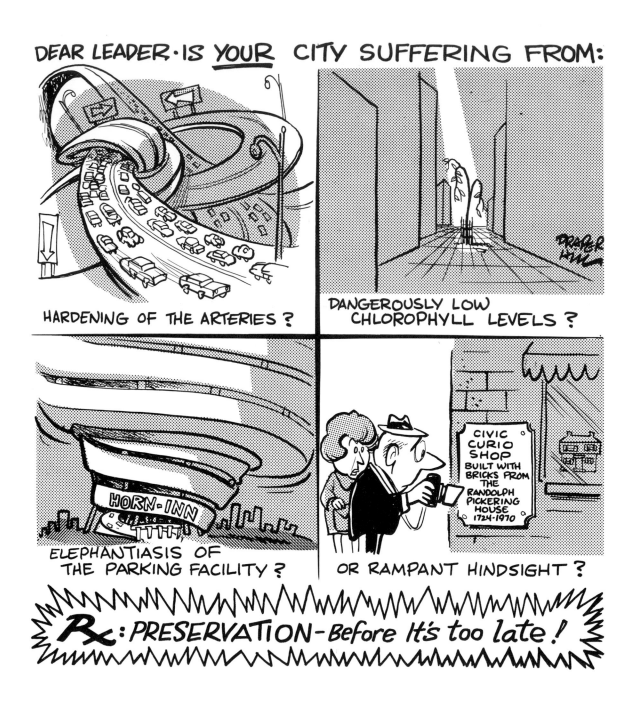

Drawing by Draper Hill; Preservation News, April 1971

Drawing by Draper Hill; Preservation News, March 1973

Wanted: A Better Mousetrap

Drawing by Draper Hill; Preservation News, May 1969

"Have they no shame?"

"Isn't the committee rushing things a little?"

"Does it look too tacked-on?

Drawing by Ned Riddle; © 1963 Reprinted by permission of General Features Corporation

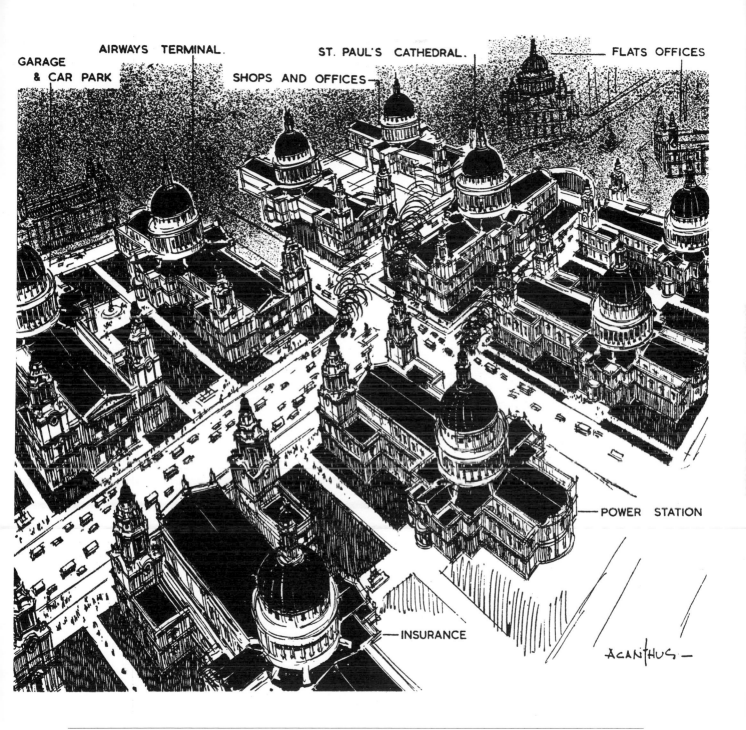

GARAGE & CAR PARK

AIRWAYS TERMINAL.

SHOPS AND OFFICES

ST. PAUL'S CATHEDRAL.

FLATS OFFICES

POWER STATION

INSURANCE

ACANTHUS

Drawing by Acanthus; © 1953 Punch, London — Rothco

"Sometimes, Carstairs, I wonder if it's worth it."

"This neighborhood sure has changed since I was a kid."

Drawing by B. Tobey; Copr. 1956 The New Yorker Magazine, Inc.

"No, I refused to be bought out; you see, I was fond
of the place and its surroundings."

Drawing by Fougasse; © 1932 Punch, London—Rothco

"Well, there goes the neighborhood."

Drawing by Jim Yanagisawa; © 1973 Planning magazine (American Society of Planning Officials), December

"All the money we've loaned them—wouldn't you think
they'd fix up the place?"

"My God! 51% of our shares have fallen into the hands of preservationists!"

"One thing I can promise you, son—none of our developments will have preservation designations placed on them."

"In a way, I hate to do it. That's one of the finest examples of twelfth-century fortified Norman."

"Another monstrosity."

Drawing by Donald Reilly; © 1969 Look magazine, February 18

". . . But it's the key to successful urban planning, ladies! . . .
We tear down the eyesores before they become historic!"

"Do you serve meals here, or is this just a shrine?"

BIDDIE AND BERT

"Makes a man proud to think that some day, on this very spot, a great community of hot dog and souvenir stands will arise!"

"At last my speed reading course is paying off . . . I can now read an historical marker without slowing down!"

Drawing by Draper Hill; Preservation News, April 1974

"When I built this house in 1865, I didn't intend for a couple of
vegetarian yahoos to come along and fill it up with plastic furniture."

Drawing by Richard Guindon; © 1974 Reprinted by permission of the Minneapolis (Minn.) Tribune, December 22

"But we couldn't have a modern house! Oh, no!
Modern was too extreme for us!"

"Got it!"

"Of course I fed it the right data—Call IBM and hurry!"

Drawing by Alan Dunn; From *Architecture Observed,* © 1971 Architectural Record Books

Drawing by Draper Hill; Preservation News, January 1974

"Leave it to the Landmarks Commission! They think of everything!"

Homesteading

Drawing by Draper Hill; Preservation News, November 1973

OUR SUBJECT TODAY IS **URBAN ARCHITECTURE** OF THE NINETEENTH AND TWENTIETH CENTURIES—BASED ON EXCAVATION AND RECONSTRUCTION OF THE RUINS OF THAT PERIOD IN HISTORY.

OF COURSE, WITH THE EVIDENCE OF SO MUCH TOTAL DESTRUCTION WE ASSUMED THE RUINS WERE CREATED BY **WAR**— UNTIL A CHANCE DISCOVERY OF A HIDDEN DOCUMENT PROVED THAT IT WASN'T WAR AT ALL — IT WAS A **GUERILLA** INSURRECTION—SOMETHING CALLED "**URBAN RENEWAL**"

OUR FIRST SLIDE SHOWS A RECONSTRUCTION OF THE EARLIEST AND MOST **PRIMITIVE** FORM OF THAT PERIOD—THE **GLASS SLAB**—BUILT PROBABLY IN THE MIDDLE NINETEENTH CENTURY— NOTICE ITS **VACUOUSNESS** AND LACK OF SCALE.

NEXT WE HAVE A **LATER**, MORE **TRANSITIONAL** HOUSE OF THE EARLY TWENTIETH CENTURY— **STILL** RATHER MONOTONOUS BUT FEATURING GREATER SOPHISTICATION OF **DETAIL**. THE RECORDS WE FOUND PROVE THAT THESE CONSTRUCTIONS WERE AT FIRST KNOWN AS "**HOUSING PROJECTS**" A CLUMSY TERM LATER SIMPLIFIED INTO "SLUMS."

OUR **LAST** SLIDE REPRESENTS A **HIGH** POINT OF PROGRESS. BUILT IN THE LATE TWENTIETH OR EARLY TWENTY-FIRST CENTURY THIS BUILDING KNOWN AS A "**BROWNSTONE**" UTILIZES A TASTE AND A FLAIR FOR EXPERIMENTATION THAT SUGGEST AN ARCHITECTURAL RENAISSANCE.

ONE CAN ONLY BE LEFT BREATHLESS BY THE BRILLIANCE OF A SOCIETY THAT WAS ABLE TO MAKE SUCH GIANT STRIDES IN A MERE ONE-HUNDRED FIFTY YEARS.

"Our preservation of the past is a responsibility to the future." —Christopher Tunnard

Drawing by Paul R. Hoffmaster; Preservation News, April 1967

"If an old herd of cows could lay out Boston . . ."

Drawing by Draper Hill; Preservation News, June 1968

"That shows a complete disregard for master planning!"

"I underestimated the power of the highway lobby in this state."

Drawing by Draper Hill; Preservation News, January 1973

Drawing by Henry R. Martin; Preservation News, June 1973

Drawing by Draper Hill; Worcester (Mass.) Telegram, March 26, 1968

HISTORIC
WILLIAMSBURG
PARKING
1 HOUR - 10 CENTS

Drawing by Alan Dunn; From *Architecture Observed*, © 1971 Architectural Record Books

Drawing by Draper Hill; Preservation News, July 1974

Drawing by Mike Peters; Dayton (Ohio) Daily News, January 2, 1972

*"Cleared with the state, cleared with the county, cleared with the
zoning boys, the building boys, the historical society, the ecology groups,
and now the little old lady changes her mind about selling
the farm."*

GREAT
URBAN
SPRAWL

W Miller

III

"*Progress was OK. It just went on too long.*" —OGDEN NASH

Overton Park, Memphis, Tenn.

Overton Park, a wooded recreational area in downtown Memphis, described by Michael Frome, writing in *American Forests*, as one of the "finest urban forests in the world," has been threatened since 1957 with bisection by a federally funded, through-town expressway, an extension of Interstate 40. Years of public hearings, court battles, judicial decisions and remanding of decisions leave the fate of the park uncertain. The Citizens to Preserve Overton Park, a citizens group that has long spearheaded the drive to save the parkland, has been aided by five National Trust matching consultant service grants. The committee's tireless efforts for the last 18 years have thus far preserved the park, but preservationists are still struggling against the encroaching highway whose pavement has been laid to the park edges. Despite continuing citizen pleas for preservation of the open space, Tennessee officials hope that in 1975 the U. S. Congress will approve legislation that will exempt the highway construction from certain environmental protection laws and provide funds to complete the interstate through Overton Park.

"Now, Henry, there's this park down in Memphis, Tennessee . . ."

Drawing by Draper Hill; The Commercial Appeal (Memphis, Tenn.), January 26, 1973

M. MARCEL MARCEAU, A DISTINGUISHED VISITOR IN TOWN, HAS GRACIOUSLY VOLUNTEERED A PROGRESS REPORT ON I-40 THROUGH OVERTON PARK...

Drawing by Draper Hill; The Commercial Appeal (Memphis, Tenn.), February 1, 1975

Extension of the West Front of the U.S. Capitol, Washington, D.C.

For years, redesign and extension of the West Front of the U. S. Capitol has been an imminent possibility. Specifically exempted (along with the Supreme Court Building and White House) from protection under the National Historic Preservation Act of 1966, the Capitol and related buildings and grounds are therefore also exempted from listing in the National Register of Historic Places. Thus, federal lawmakers can vote to change the historic structure at any time and their decision is not subject to review by the Advisory Council on Historic Preservation. Normally, this review procedure is mandatory for national, state and local landmarks listed in the National Register and affected by federally funded projects. The West Front is the only remaining exterior portion of the building that retains 18th and 19th-century elements designed by William Thornton, Benjamin H. Latrobe and Charles Bulfinch; redesign of this Capitol facade would also destroy the western terraces designed by Frederick Law Olmsted.

In 1966, a proposal was made to extend the West Front, but it was defeated. However, in 1969, a proposal for the extension met with approval in the House of Representatives and $2 million was appropriated to prepare contract specifications. Public outcry against the proposal was led by the American Institute of Architects. The National Trust, joining the protest, cited the Historic Sites Act of 1935 and the National Historic Preservation Act of 1966, both of which define a national policy of preservation of historic and cultural sites and buildings. Although the 1969 proposal was put aside after a congressionally commissioned study by a New York engineering firm proved the soundness of the historic walls in 1971, some legislators have continued to call for the extension and to present bills proposing the redesign in nearly every session of Congress since 1969.

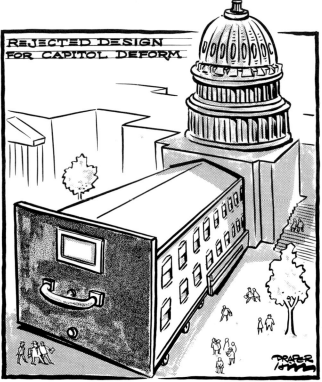

Westward No!

Drawing by Draper Hill; Preservation News, February 1971

"Where did you get the idea you have anything to say about it?"

Drawing by Herblock; From *The Herblock Gallery*, © 1968 Simon and Schuster

Pennsylvania Station, New York City

Protests against demolition of the New York City Pennsylvania Station in the mid-1960s failed to save the terminal whose nobility and grandeur of design were considered by architectural historians to be unequaled by any other station in the world. The 1906 Charles F. McKim design was based on the Roman Baths of Caracalla; with its Roman Doric facade and vaulted ceilings, the station was called the greatest monument to the empire of the American railroad. Opposition to construction of the new Madison Square Garden, bowling alley, hotel and highrise office complex that replaced the historic station was led by such respected figures and organizations as Aline Saarinen, Philip Johnson, Peter Blake, the Museum of Modern Art, the Columbia University School of Architecture, Lewis Mumford, the Pratt Institute School of Architecture,

Alfred Knopf and the National Trust. Additional opposition from the *New Yorker* and *Life* magazines and the *New York Times* failed to sway the city council from its decision to permit demolition of the famous station.

By 1966, the station was a tumble of shattered Corinthian columns, cracked marble and twisted steel, lying in a landfill in a New Jersey meadow. Yet even the demolition of the station has historical significance to preservationists: It was the loss of this building, along with the Brokaw House, that led to the enactment of the New York City landmarks law and the establishment of the New York City Landmarks Preservation Commission.

Drawing by Alan Dunn; From *Architecture Observed*, © 1971 Architectural Record Books

Grand Central Station, New York City

Recent plans for the demolition, defacement or redesign of Grand Central Station in New York City have met with protest from preservationists. Designed in 1913 by architects Warren & Wetmore and Reed & Stem, the Beaux Arts–style station is described by architect Hugh Hardy as a "unique combination of commercial, transportation, entertainment, residential and recreational activities" and as a "symbol, marketplace and economic engine with which a preeminently important part of midtown Manhattan can be rejuvenated." In 1961, the first proposal to enable the building to bring in more income—horizontally dividing the vast waiting room into four floors of bowling alleys—was thwarted. In 1967, the terminal was designated a city landmark and in March 1975 it was listed in the National Register of Historic Places. In 1969, the existence of the station was threatened by plans to erect a 55-story office tower over the 42nd street end of the terminal.

Twice since the plans were announced, the New York City Landmarks Preservation Commission, which must pass on proposed changes to the exteriors of city landmarks, has denied a certificate of no exterior effect, preventing the applicants—Penn Central, UGP, Ltd., of London, the New York and Harlem Railroad Company and the 51st Street Realty Corporation—from constructing the new skyscraper. When the applicants appealed their case to the Supreme Court of New York County, Justice Irving H. Saypol, in January 1975 invalidated the building's landmark status, thus releasing the owners from building restrictions protecting landmarks. He declared that the prevention of Penn Central plans to build the office tower would result in an economic hardship on the bankrupt company and would constitute a taking of property. An 88-member Committee to Save Grand Central Station, headed by former Mayor Robert F. Wagner and including Philip Johnson and Jacqueline Kennedy Onassis, was quickly formed to oppose the defacement of the terminal, and the city announced plans to appeal the ruling. Supporting preservation of the terminal are the American Institute of Architects and the National Trust, which earlier was a party to an *amicus curiae* brief on defense of the terminal's landmark designation. Justice Saypol's decision dealt the preservation movement a temporary setback, but the appeal could yet result in victory for the New York City Landmarks Preservation Commission and the Committee to Save Grand Central Station.

Drawing by Draper Hill; Preservation News, March 1975

St. Louis Post Office, St. Louis, Mo.

In 1959, the U. S. General Services Administration announced plans to vacate the old St. Louis Post Office and erect a new highrise office building on its site. Designed in 1872 by Alfred B. Mullet, architect of federal buildings, the French Second Empire-style structure is generally acknowledged to be one of the finest post office buildings remaining from the era immediately following the Civil War. It was listed in the National Register of Historic Places in 1968 and designated a National Historic Landmark in 1971. Public interest in the historic structure encouraged the federal government to lease new office space rather than immediately make plans to replace the post office, but for years there was indecision about whether to preserve or dispose of the building. Local citizens groups, including the St. Louis Artists Guild, the Committee to Save the Old Post Office and the Landmarks Association of St. Louis, with the support of the Society of Architectural Historians, the American Institute of Architects, the American Institute of Interior Designers and the National Trust, waged a 16-year battle for its preservation.

By 1970, several studies had been made and many people agreed that the best plan for preserving the building required adaptive commercial use. This was the first time the adaptation of a federally owned architectural monument for other than museum or government use was seriously suggested. With this building as the primary case, an amendment to the Federal Property and Administrative Services Act of 1949 was passed in 1972. Called the Old Post Office Bill, the amendment provides for the transfer of historically important surplus public buildings to states or municipalities at no cost and permits their use for revenue-producing functions. Formerly, reuse of such buildings was restricted to museum or other noncommercial purposes. A private development firm, aided by funds made available by the National Trust, the National Park Service and the Landmarks Association of St. Louis, is

Eagle Roost

currently updating its plans and projections for restoration and adaptation of the post office as a hotel and for other commercial uses. In addition, the General Services Administration is studying the possibility of restoration and renovation for new federal occupancy.

Drawing by Thos. A. Englehardt; St. Louis (Mo.) Post-Dispatch, January 12, 1971

Chicago Stock Exchange, Chicago, Ill.

The 1893 Chicago Stock Exchange, considered one of the most important achievements of Chicago School architects Adler and Sullivan, was relinquished to the wrecking ball in October 1971. The Chicago City Council had refused to award the historic structure protective designation as a city landmark, and court battles, economic development proposals, new legislation, fund-raising drives and editorial appeals failed to rescue the building. Pleas came from the Commission on Chicago Historical and Architectural Landmarks and support from many individuals and organizations, including the Landmarks Preservation Council, the Chicago chapter of the American Institute of Architects, the American Institute of Planners, the Society of Architectural Historians, the Metropolitan Housing Council, the Advisory Council on Historic Preservation and the National Trust. The efforts were to no avail, except that some architectural details were saved by various preservation and museum groups.

Although the Stock Exchange was lost, the battle provided the impetus for a study of development rights transfers. Funds from the AIA Chicago Chapter Foundation, the National Trust and the U.S. Department of Housing and Urban Development for studies by John J. Costonis culminated in publication of the book, *Space Adrift*.

Four years after the exchange building was destroyed, an ironic note was sounded when in March 1975 the developers who demolished the 13-story structure sought court approval for financial reorganization, claiming that their 43-story replacement building was economically unviable.

"If it weren't for us the city would be cluttered with architectural masterpieces."

Diamond Head, Honolulu, Hawaii

"Good Grief, YOU Again?"

In 1969, millionaire land developer Chinn Ho announced plans to construct highrise hotels and apartments on the seaward slopes of Hawaii's historic Diamond Head. For centuries, this volcanic mountain overlooking Honolulu welcomed voyagers to the island; its slopes contain mica deposits which, when struck by the sun, shine like diamonds over the harbor. The mountain was a holy place to early Hawaiians and sacred temples were built there.

Chinn Ho failed to gain development permission when citizens, business groups and the *Honolulu Advertiser* organized a lengthy and successful opposition to the plan. Although the efforts of the Diamond Head preservationists were supported by the governor of Hawaii, the National Trust and the U. S. Departments of the Interior and Housing and Urban Development, eight years of negotiations were required before the mountain was declared a national Natural Landmark, protective zoning was enacted and the future of its seaward face assured as a public park.

Drawing by Harry Lyons; Honolulu (Hawaii) Advertiser, April 5, 1967

National Gettysburg Battlefield Tower, Gettysburg, Pa.

In spite of a preservation effort led by Pennsylvania Gov. Milton J. Shapp and Atty. Gen. J. Shane Creamer, the Pennsylvania Supreme Court ruled on October 5, 1973, in favor of Maryland businessman Thomas R. Ottenstein's plan to build an observation tower at the site of the pivotal battle of the Civil War. As planned, the tower was to loom high above the ground where the Battle of Gettysburg was fought in 1863 and where Abraham Lincoln delivered his eloquent "Gettysburg Address."

Joining the state leaders and other Pennsylvania preservationists in opposition to the tower was the Advisory Council on Historic Preservation. The recommendations of the council and pleas by New York State and the U. S. Department of the Interior also failed to halt the construction. The strip of commercial development—motels, souvenir stands and fast-food marts—that proliferated in the area before the tower was built and the lack of protective zoning ordinances that made this sort of commercial enterprise possible also meant that there was little environmental basis on which to fight the tower proposition.

The tower, completed in 1974, now offers tourists a view of the battleground from a height of 307 feet.

Drawing by Tony Auth; Philadelphia (Pa.) Inquirer, February 21, 1973

Green Springs, Va.

On March 1, 1973, the Green Springs historic district was listed in the National Register of Historic Places. The first rural historic district, it is also the largest, covering 640 acres and containing more than 30 individual landmarks. In 1970, however, only three of the distinctive 18th and 19th-century houses were listed in the Register, and the historic rural town was threatened by plans to construct a new state penitentiary on a site directly across from an 1851 Tuscan villa designed by Alexander Jackson Davis. The area contains outstanding examples of architecture preserved in their original context, and among these examples the evolution of the Virginia house from 1740 to 1860 can be traced. The proposed prison facility would have occupied 12 percent of the land area of Green Springs.

Preservationists faced years of court battles, conflicting environmental impact statements and opposition forces led by Gov. A. Linwood Holton, Jr., who seemed determined to place the penal facility in their midst. In the complex struggle, the Green Springs Association was supported by a National Trust matching consultant service grant and by Trust aid in litigation procedures. Support came also from Rogers C. B. Morton, Secretary of the Interior, and from Governor Holton's successor, Mills E. Godwin. On June 13, 1974, opponents of the prison construction celebrated victory when Governor Godwin made a final pronouncement that the prison would not be located in Green Springs.

Throughout the struggle against the prison, preservation efforts were complicated by the separate threat of strip-mining operations by the firm of W. R. Grace & Company. This threat continues: In April 1975, W. R. Grace was granted approval for a zoning exception for a portion of its holdings, allowing the company to proceed with mining operations on 800 acres in Green Springs.

Executive Clemency

Drawing by Draper Hill; Preservation News, November 1972

Index

Acanthus (Frank Hoare) 31
Addams, Charles 2
Alley, Cal xxiv
Auth, Tony 83

Bennett, C. H. xxi
Bird, Kenneth (see Fougasse)
Block, Herbert (see Herblock)
Booth, George 68
Brewster, Elizabeth F. 73
Brummer, F. H. 22
Burck, Jacob 81
Burgin, Eric 43

Censoni, Robert 32
Cobean, Sam 50
Cruikshank, George xviii-xix

Day, Chon 72
Day, Robert viii, 17
Donovan, Bob 45
Dunn, Alan 3, 13, 51, 52, 54, 65, 78, 86
Dunn, Louis 1

Englehardt, Thomas A. 80

Feiffer, Jules 56
Folger, Franklin 37
Fougasse (Kenneth Bird) xxv, 35
Fradon, Dana 27

Gerard, David C. 15
Guindon, Richard 49

Hamilton, William 69
Herblock (Herbert Block) 77
Hill, Draper 10, 18, 21, 24, 25, 26,
    48, 53, 55, 58, 61, 63, 66, 74, 75, 76,
    79, 85
Hoare, Frank (see Acanthus)
Hoffmaster, Paul R. v, 57
Hokinson, Helen E. 44
Holland, John 38, 39
Honeysett, Martin 33

Interpress Film 16

Keate, Jeff 20

Lichty, George 23, 28, 42, 46, 47, 59
Lyons, Harry 82

Martin, Henry R. 9, 62
Miller, Warren 70-71
Mulligan, James 12
Myers, David 6

O'Glass, Charles E. 30

Peters, Mike 67
Price, Garrett 8

Reilly, Donald 41
Reinhart, Charles Stanley xii
Renault, Dennis 5

Riddle, Ned 29
Ruge, John 11

Saxon, Charles cover
Schneider, Howie 14
Schochet, Bob 4
Schulz, Charles 64
Stevenson, James 40, 60
Sullivan, J. F. xxii

Tobey, Barney 34

Vietor, Dean 19

Williams, Gluyas xv
Wilson, Rowland B. 7

Yanagisawa, Jim 36

Drawing by Alan Dunn; Copr. 1936, 1964 The New Yorker Magazine, Inc.